ESSENTIAL
VANCOUVER &
THE CANADIAN
ROCKIES

★ Best places to see 34–55   ■ Featured sight

Written by Tim Jepson
Verified by Des Hannigan

© AA Media Limited 2009
First published 2009

ISBN: 978-0-7495-6250-2

Published by AA Publishing, a trading name of AA Media Limited, whose registered
office is Fanum House, Basing View, Basingstoke, Hampshire RG21 4EA.
Registered number 06112600.

Colour separation: MRM Graphics Ltd
Printed and bound in Italy by Printer Trento S.r.l.

A03808
Mapping in this title produced from map data supplied by Global Mapping, Brackley,
UK. Copyright © Global Mapping/ITMB